TIME RELEASE POEMS

To Allan

– Respect!

Robert Priest

1998

TIME RELEASE POEMS

robert priest

Canadian Cataloguing in Publication Data

Priest, Robert
Time release poems

ISBN 1-896860-17-6

I. Title.
PS8581.R47T56 1997 C811'.54 C97-910869-1
PR9199.3.SP745T56 1997

Cover, photo and sculpture: Miles Lowry

Published in 1997 by
Ekstasis Editions Canada Ltd.
Box 8474, Main Postal Outlet
Victoria, B.C. V8W 3S1

EkstasisEdition
Box 57
Banff, Alberta T0L 0C

Most of the sayings have been printed in these earlier books: *Sadness* *Spacemen* (Dreadnaught), *The Man Who Broke Out of the Letter* (CoachHouse Press), *The Mad Hand* (CoachHouse Press), *Scream Blu* *Living* (The Mercury Press), and *Resurrection in the Cartoon* (ECW Press). musical version of some this book is available on the CD *Tongue 'N' Groov* (EMI/Artisan).

The author would like to thank the following Arts Councils fo various grants which helped in the writing of ***Time Release Poems***: Th Ontario Arts Council, The Toronto Arts Council, The Canada Council.

Time Release Poems has been published with the assistance of a grar from the Canada Council and the Cultural Services Branch of Britis Columbia.

TIME RELEASE POEMS

✪✪✪

To Frank and Lynda Davies....
& to the Memory of Judy Merrill

Thanks to Marsha Kirzner
for her love and help

Different destinations
but for a while the same path.

Sometimes it is the book that opens you.

No matter which way you turn
there's always something you're not facing.

Whitewash comes in many colours.

Busy is the man with many hats
and nothing to put them on.

There is no peace for the punching bag.

True marksmen see beyond guns.

Too much time is wasted
in the making of clocks.

Every little ruler wants a 13th inch.

There is no camouflage
like a good philosophy.

Cars —
people fleeing *in* their problems.

Everything leads
to everything else.

The teacher *is* the lesson.

A little bit of knowledge is
a beginning.

Never say "Never say never."

When you deny
you deny you deny
When you deny you deny
you deny you deny you deny
when you deny you deny you deny
you deny you deny you deny you deny!

You can't go down from the bottom.

There is no trampoline
like the bottom of the soul.

The edge comes from within.

Home is where the heat is.

There is nothing so efficient
as the last match.

It is easiest to fast
just after eating.

If the sickness don't get you the cure will.

If the famine don't get you the feast will.

If the thirst don't get you the water will.

If the celibacy don't get you —

Good lovers come in pairs.

Every love is a victory.

The hotter the sun
the quicker the honey.

There is no balance without opposition.

You cannot kiss ass and kick it too.

You can't murder the dead.

The most dangerous people are the obedient.

Quislings with no Reich!

The only thing they hate more than ambition is success.

Watch out they don't knock your head off
when they're patting you on the back.

To cut bread with a dagger.

To fear the gun and butter too.

To break one egg on another.

To carry an egg in too many baskets.

Inflation —
the increasing cost of our unhappiness.

The knife will not soften
for the throat.

Clothes make the man
— poor.

A hole in a dime
the size of a dime.

To blow out the match and the candle too.

Don't call your own shadow the night.

When the last light goes out
what is the speed of darkness?

Are you ready for the euthanasia
—*YET!*

Don't love the rose only for its thorns.

Don't sharpen the arrow as it hits you.

It is the edge that makes the knife.

That is like setting yourself on fire
in order to see in the dark.

To read by the light of burning pianos.

To burn a good cook.

To hide a pin prick in a sword's thrust.

To cry for the thirsty.

It is the stomach that makes a strong back.

Even the wicked love songs of joy.

Take your time
— just don't take mine

Go the lighted ways...

Catch a falling star
— sometimes you burn your hand

Can I touch it with my cane?

Why do the forgiven talk so softly?

The apology is never as loud as the insult.

In the wrong hands even doves are dangerous.

Don't give a good message a bad name.

The loudest music on earth advises —
"Listen to your heart!"

The rotweiller pacifists!
The rotweiller pacifists!

Any grain of sand can make a pearl.

You can't repair a fallen leaf.

If you would see a parent
look in the eyes of the child.

The truth is trying to find you.

Dust loves a dry throat.

Honey hates a sweet voice.

Save something
or get off the cross.

Forgive and remember.

The parentarchy...

Hurricanes at home move faraway sails.

Do you travel for the journey
or just for the arrival?

People begin as dreams and end as memories.

A day is only as bright as the people in it.

Dreams have a kind of gravity
drawing the real to a new reality.

You do not go to find clarity in the clouds.

You can't make tea without water.
(*Marsha Kirzner*)

You can't forgive yourself
without forgiving others.

A sweet tongue won't cure a rotten tooth.

One crumb is a hook to another crumb
and you can never go anywhere
but to another crumb
and there are advertisements on the way
all for a 'better crumb'
and you can never have the whole loaf.

Serious times breed comedians.

To laugh at your own teeth.

Get it off your chest
and onto your conscience.

Though the candle is crooked
the flame is still straight.

There is nothing worse for men
than overcoming giants.

Sometimes the shadow is bigger
than the cat.

If you change either
you change the other.

Beware of the cautious...

Be bold
or be bowled over.

You get bitter
and then you get better.
(*with P. Lafferty*)

Sometimes being mixed up makes the cake.

There is no neck
like the head itself.

Don't blame the mirror
for your face.

All package no content.

All edge no interior.

All interior no edge —
(infinity).

The last number is affinity.
(*Eli Kirzner-Priest —age 4*)

One tooth works with another.

Every tooth affects the bite.

Every turn of the wheel
sharpens the knife.

Every little drop
makes the rain.

If you want to bounce
you've got to hit the bottom.

A fool will always find
banana skins.

A fool cannot tell a pie
from a face cloth.

No one is too stupid
to be a Fool.

There is nothing to stop a fool
from becoming a high school teacher.

There are fools even among the wise.

A fool may live with a wise man
a thousand years and still know nothing.

Maybe we've got nothing
but nothing lasts forever.

You cannot avoid the void.

You cannot refuse the rain.

The arrow is fastest
just before it strikes.

Stop procrastinating
— tomorrow!

I can't wait
to be patient.

The injustice system.

Resolution not revolution.

✪ ✪ ✪

The peace you make may be your own.

✪ ✪ ✪

Not just PEACE but a JUST peace.

The only peace is JUSTICE.

Justice not justification.

We're bigger than all of us.

I can see the planet in your eyes.

The only promise is doing.

One wind moves many flags.

Daylight respects no borders

A paradise for all is a fool's paradise too.

Looking won't make it come.

"Make a list of your wildest hopes!"
— Marsha Kirzner

✪ ✪ ✪

Only the loudest voice of all can obtain it —
SILENCE!